THE CHIPPY TOUR

CHIPPY

RECIPES

SJP

thechippytour.com

Mission Statement for The Chippy Tour

At The Chippy Tour, my mission is to champion the legacy and allure of traditional fish and chip shops across the United Kingdom and beyond. I am dedicated to cultivating a global appreciation for this culinary experience by sharing authentic recipes and stories that celebrate the rich heritage of the chip shop.

My goal is to inspire food enthusiasts everywhere to discover the unique flavours and communal joy found in traditional chippies. By providing insights into the artistry behind the fryer, I aim to encourage a deeper understanding and respect for these beloved institutions, prompting more people to explore and support local fish and chip shops.

Through my endeavours, I aspire to preserve the chip shop's tradition and spread its comforting, classic taste to every corner of the world.

As a successful home chef with several bestselling recipe books to my name, I've channelled that expertise into the creation of this book and The Chippy Tour. To spread awareness about the importance of preserving traditional fish and chip shops, I've made this book as affordable as possible, aiming to inspire support and ensure that traditional chippies continue to flourish.

Website:	thechippytour.com
YouTube Channel:	youtube.com/@chippytour
Instagram (Food Highlights):	instagram.com/thechippytour_uk
Facebook:	facebook.com/groups/thechippytour
TikTok (Food Highlights):	tiktok.com/@thechippytour
X:	twitter.com/thechippytour

The Chippy Tour Chippy Recipes
A Culinary Adventure Through Fish and Chip Shop Recipes

Dive into the heart of Britain's beloved culinary tradition with "The Chippy Tour Chippy Recipes" recipe book, your ultimate guide to mastering the art of the perfect fish and chips. From the crispy, golden batter that encases succulently tender fish to a plethora of popular chippy items, this book is a treasure trove of recipes that promises to elevate your cooking game and bring a taste of the finest fish and chip shops into your kitchen.

But "The Chippy Tour Chippy Recipes" is more than just a cookbook; it's an invitation to embark on a journey through the history, techniques, and secrets behind creating the perfect chippy meal. Each page contains delicious recipes.

Are you craving more? The adventure doesn't stop at the book. Visit The Chippy Tour website and YouTube channel for an experience featuring video reviews of fish and chip shops across the country. Discover hidden gems, and join a community of enthusiasts passionate about celebrating and preserving this iconic dish. The website contains blogs and other helpful resources to enrich your culinary exploration.

Whether you're a seasoned cook looking to refine your skills or eager to discover the joys of chippy dishes, "The Chippy Tour Chippy Recipes" book and website offer everything you need to create mouthwatering meals and make lasting memories. So, tie on your apron, heat your fryer, and prepare to embark on a delicious adventure with "The Chippy Tour."

Achieving the distinctive flavour of traditional chip shop batter at home is challenging, mainly because the oil or fat used in chippies has typically cooked a variety of items. This includes fish, sausages, burgers, chips, savouries, fish cakes, and even the odd chocolate bar, contributing to the unique taste. Despite the batter's basic ingredients, nothing matches the chippy experience.

Nonetheless, preparing fish, meats, and chips in various tasty batters at home is certainly a wonderful idea if getting to a chippy for whatever reason is not possible. Cooking at home also helps with dietary preferences and requirements, such as vegetarian, vegan, allergy-friendly, or gluten-free.

Note

These recipes are designed to be adaptable to your personal preferences. I provide recommended amounts for ingredients, but you are encouraged to modify these to suit your taste, for example, by reducing the batter quantity when cooking fewer fillets. I will suggest different ingredients that work well with the same batter. You can season with salt and pepper to your liking, choose the oil or fat you prefer, and select your own cooking method. I've discovered and recommend heating the oil or fat to 190C/370F for optimal deep-frying results.

Throughout this book, you'll find that batter recipes typically require coating the items in flour, followed by a batter before frying. On the other hand, recipes that use breadcrumbs generally involve dredging the items in flour, dipping them in beaten eggs, and coating them in breadcrumbs. This process ensures that the breadcrumbs adhere properly, as the flour and egg create a sticky base that acts like a thin batter.

I have provided measurements in both metric and imperial units, as well as spoon and cup measurements. This accommodates those who use a mix of these units and will help people worldwide.

Pies and pasties are not included in the recipes due to the vast majority of chippies buying them in from reputable suppliers.

Recipes

These recipes can be easily tailored to your tastes. Ingredient quantities are suggested, but feel free to adjust them, such as halving the batter for fewer fillets. The same batter works well with various ingredients, which we'll mention throughout. Seasoning with salt and pepper, choosing your preferred oil, and selecting cooking methods like deep frying or baking are all up to personal preference. I also prefer the oil or fat at 180C/370F for deep frying, though you may prefer another heat setting based on the oil or fat you prefer.

EXPLORING THE HISTORY OF FISH AND CHIPS

It's a classic dish that generations have enjoyed. But have you ever wondered about the history behind this beloved meal?

The roots of fish and chips can be traced back to the 19th century when the dish was first introduced to the working-class communities of England. It was a simple and affordable meal that provided sustenance to the working class, who often lived in poverty-stricken areas. It was said to originate from Jewish families in Portugal and Spain before they migrated to the UK and worldwide.

Fish and chips quickly became a staple food for these communities, offering families a cheap and filling option. The combination of fish and chips was a marriage of convenience. Fish was readily available and inexpensive, thanks to the thriving fishing industry in coastal towns. On the other hand, potatoes were an affordable and abundant crop that could be easily turned into chips.

The two ingredients came together to create a delicious and satisfying meal. As the popularity of fish and chips grew, so did the number of fish and chip shops. These establishments became a community hub, serving as a gathering place for friends and families to enjoy eating together. The fish and chip shop became an integral part of British culture, with its distinctive aroma and bustling atmosphere.

Over the years, fish and chips have evolved and adapted to changing tastes and preferences. Different regions in the UK and countries worldwide have dish variations, with some using different types of fish or batter. The versatility of fish and chips has allowed it to remain a beloved dish.

So, the next time you sit down to enjoy a plate of fish and chips, take a moment to appreciate the history and tradition behind this iconic dish. And remember, by supporting your local fish and chip shop, you're satisfying your taste buds and helping preserve a piece of British culinary heritage. It can also be satisfying and cost-effective to cook many fish and chip shop favourites at home, which is why I have published this book.

BATTER AND WHY FISH AND CHIP SHOPS ARE SO POPULAR

The irresistible appeal of battered foods from fish and chip shops can be attributed to several factors that tickle the taste buds and draw crowds:

Texture Contrast: Combining a crispy, golden batter against the soft, moist interior of a fish, a burger, or a sausage provides a satisfying contrast in textures. This contrast is a key element that makes battered food appealing.

Flavourful Batter: The batter, often a simple mix of flour, salt, and water, can also include beer, milk and other products to add a distinct flavour. When seasoned correctly and fried at the perfect temperature, it has a delicious taste that complements the food.

Comfort Food: There's an inherent comfort in indulging in warm, fried foods. For many, it evokes nostalgia and provides a sense of indulgence and satisfaction that is hard to replicate with other cooking methods.

The Maillard Reaction: The process of frying creates the Maillard reaction, which occurs when the proteins and sugars in the batter turn golden brown and develop a rich array of flavours. This chemical reaction is responsible for fried foods' tempting aroma and taste.

Social and Cultural Aspect: Fish and chip shops are often social hubs in local communities, where people gather and enjoy traditional food that has been part of British culture for generations. They are not just selling food; they offer an experience, often including communal sharing and enjoyment.

<u>Variety and Novelty:</u> The trend of battering and frying various foods, from traditional fish and sausages to chocolate bars and even ice cream, means there's always something new and exciting to try. This novelty factor can attract people who are eager to experience the latest deep-fried creation.

<u>The Indulgence Factor:</u> Let's face it: indulging in deep-fried foods is often a treat. The fact that these foods are not something one should eat daily makes them even more tempting as an occasional splurge.

The tastiness of battered foods from fish and chip shops comes down to the perfect blend of textures, flavours, and the sense of comfort and community these establishments provide. These factors, combined with the novelty and sheer indulgence of it all, keep people flocking to them.

BESIDES FISH, WHAT GETS BATTERED AND WHAT IS THE MAILLARD REACTION?

We will create some delicious battered food recipes in this publication, such as battered sausages, burgers, fruit, and more, but what about the deep-fried chocolate phenomenon, and why should you try it?

Novelty: Trying unconventional food combinations can be a fun experience. Deep-fried chocolate stands out because it's unexpected and different from traditional savoury fried items.

Texture Contrast: The batter's crispness contrasts with the chocolate's melted, gooey interior, which can be a delightful sensory experience.

Indulgence: Deep-fried chocolate is an indulgent treat appealing to those looking for a decadent dessert.

Fairground and Festival Culture: The practice mirrors the food often found at fairs and festivals, where deep-fried sweets are popular. Fish and chip shops may offer these items to capture that sense of enjoyment and festivity.

Media and Virality: Social media plays a significant role in spreading food fads. Deep-fried chocolate is visually exciting and tends to attract attention, making it more likely to be shared online.

Curiosity and One-upmanship: There's also a competitive edge to the trend, with shops and customers alike curious to see who can create the most outlandish deep-fried creation.

Culinary Hybridisation: Combining elements of traditional fish and chips with the universal appeal of chocolate creates a unique hybrid that can attract traditional customers and those seeking something new.

While not for everyone, the fad of deep-frying sweet items like chocolate in fish and chip shops caters to adventurous eaters and those looking to indulge in a unique, once-in-a-while treat. It also adds a bit of fun and variety to the menu, distinguishing a shop from its competitors.

THE HEALTHIER SIDE OF FISH AND CHIPS

Fish and chips, a beloved British staple, often evoke images of a hearty, indulgent meal. But have you ever considered its place within a balanced diet? Let's delve into the nutritional aspects of this iconic dish, especially when enjoyed with traditional salt and vinegar.

Understanding the Calorie Content

An average portion of fish and chips contains about 900 calories. When I compare this to the daily calorie intake recommendation of 2,550 calories for men and 1,940 for women (aged 19-50 years) – fish and chips can fit into a well-balanced diet, provided the rest of the day's meals are adjusted.

The Nutritional Breakdown

Beyond calories, fish and chips offer a mix of proteins, carbohydrates, and fats. The fish, typically cod or haddock, is an excellent source of lean protein and Omega-3 fatty acids, essential for heart and brain health. The batter adds carbohydrates and some fat, while the chips contribute more carbs and fats.

Incorporating Salt and Vinegar

Salt and vinegar are more than just flavour enhancers. Vinegar, particularly malt vinegar, contains negligible calories and can help digestion. However, it's essential to be mindful of the salt content. Excessive salt can lead to increased blood pressure and other health issues. A light sprinkle can enhance the taste without overdoing the sodium intake.

Healthier Cooking Methods

Many fish and chip shops now offer grilled or baked fish as an alternative to the traditional fried option.

This cooking method significantly reduces the calorie and fat content of the meal, making it a healthier choice. Though, I'll stick to the deep-fried method for now.

Portion Control

One of the simplest ways to enjoy fish and chips healthily is to watch the portion sizes. Sharing a portion or a smaller size can make this dish a more diet-friendly option.

Balancing Your Meals

If you plan to indulge in fish and chips, consider balancing your other meals throughout the day. Opt for lighter, vegetable-rich meals that are lower in calories and high in nutrients.

Conclusion

Fish and chips can be part of a balanced diet when consumed mindfully. It's all about portion control, balancing the rest of your meals, and making healthier choices, such as vinegar over excessive salt. So, next time you're craving this quintessentially British dish, remember that it can fit into a healthy lifestyle with the right approach. Enjoy your meal responsibly and savour every bite of this timeless classic!

FRYING IN OIL VS FAT

Types of Oil and Fat

Vegetable Oils: Commonly used oils include palm oil, sunflower, canola (rapeseed), and soybean. These oils have high smoke points, making them suitable for the high-temperature frying needed for crispy fish and chips.

Animal Fats: Traditional fats like beef dripping or lard were historically used and are still favoured in some shops for their distinct flavour. Lard comes from pork and is preferred less over beef dripping at chippies.

Health Considerations

Saturated vs Unsaturated Fats: Vegetable oils are generally high in unsaturated fats and are considered healthier than saturated fats found in animal fats. Unsaturated fats can help to maintain healthy cholesterol levels.

Trans Fats: Hydrogenated vegetable oils can contain trans fats, which are unhealthy. However, many manufacturers have reduced or eliminated trans fats from their products.

Omega-3 Fatty Acids: Some oils, like canola, have omega-3 fatty acids, which are beneficial for heart health.

Heat Stability: Oils with high smoke points are less likely to break down into harmful compounds at high temperatures.

Reusability: Oils can become unhealthy if reused excessively. Degradation of oil quality over time can lead to the formation of harmful compounds.

Impact on Taste and Texture

Flavour: Animal fats can impart a richer, more traditional flavour to fish and chips but may be heavier. Vegetable oils are lighter and can allow the natural taste of the fish and potatoes to shine through.

Texture: The choice of oil can affect the crispiness of the batter and the chips. Generally, high-quality oil at the correct temperature yields a crispier texture.

Environmental and Ethical Considerations

Source: The environmental impact of production (like palm oil) is a concern. More sustainable and ethically sourced oils are increasingly in demand.

<u>Vegetarian and Vegan Preferences:</u> Vegetable oils are suitable for vegetarian and vegan diets, whereas animal fats are not.

Best Practices

<u>Temperature Control:</u> Maintaining the correct frying temperature, typically between 170C/350F to 190C/370F. I prefer to deep fry at 180C/370F, but you can experiment.

<u>Oil Filtration and Replacement:</u> Regular filtration and timely oil replacement can reduce health risks and maintain food quality. Beef dripping and lard can be used up to around 5 times, sieving out the scraps after each fry.

In conclusion, while vegetable oils are generally considered a healthier option due to lower saturated fat content and higher stability at high temperatures, the choice of oil or fat also depends on flavour preferences, tradition, and dietary considerations. Regular oil quality management is essential for health and the best culinary results.

WHICH POTATOES DO CHIPPIES USE

Fish and chip shops typically favour certain types of potatoes that are best suited for deep frying. The ideal potatoes for making chips are high in starch and low in water content, as they tend to fry better and achieve a crispy exterior while maintaining a fluffy interior.

Maris Piper: This is a popular choice for fish and chip shops. Maris Piper potatoes have a high dry matter content, making them great for frying.

King Edward: Known for their light, fluffy texture, King Edward potatoes are also a good chip choice. They have a slightly lower starch content than Maris Piper but still deliver good results.

Agria: When fried, this variety is favoured in some regions for its high starch content and golden colour.

Russet Burbank: Commonly used in the United States, Russet Burbank potatoes are high in starch and have a classic fluffy texture, making them ideal for chips.

Sagitta: These are another variety known for their suitability for chip making, offering a good balance of texture and flavour.

Fontane: This variety is increasingly popular due to its good frying qualities and lower sugar content, which reduces the likelihood of chips turning too brown when fried.

Different regions might have local preferences based on the availability and specific characteristics of potato varieties grown in the area. Fish and chip shops often choose their potatoes based on the season, as the quality and attributes of potatoes can change throughout the year.

Starch Content: Potatoes with a higher starch content, like Maris Piper and Russet Burbank, tend to absorb less oil during frying, resulting in chips that are crispy on the outside and fluffy on the inside. The starch forms a crust that encapsulates the moisture inside, cooking the potato evenly.

Sugar Content: Lower sugar content is desirable. High-sugar potatoes can lead to excessive browning or burning during frying due to the caramelisation of sugars. Varieties like Fontane are preferred for their lower sugar levels, which help achieve a golden colour without over-browning.

Dry Matter Content: Potatoes with a higher dry matter content and less water, like King Edward and Agria, fry better because they have less moisture that needs to be cooked off. This results in a less soggy, more crispy chip.

Texture and Consistency: The texture of the potato is important for the feel of the chips in the mouth. Varieties like Maris Piper and King Edward have a fluffy texture when cooked, which is highly desirable in a good chip.

Oil Retention: Some varieties are better at not absorbing too much oil. This is healthier and enhances the taste as the chip doesn't become greasy.

Seasonal Variation: Potatoes can change in quality throughout the year. For instance, new potatoes harvested early in the season might have higher water content. Fish and chip shops often adjust their potato choice based on seasonal variations to ensure consistent quality.

Regional Variations: The choice of potato can also depend on local availability and regional preferences. Certain varieties might be more popular in different parts of the UK or the world due to their local cultivation and characteristics.

Size and Shape: Lastly, the size and shape of the potato can also be a factor. Larger potatoes are often preferred as they yield bigger chips, which are popular among customers.

In conclusion, fish and chip shops invest much thought into selecting the right type of potato. The goal is always to achieve that perfect balance of a crispy exterior and a soft, fluffy interior, which makes for a delicious chip.

I TRUST YOU FOUND THIS INFORMATION INTERESTING.

NOW, LET'S CONTINUE WITH SOME WONDERFUL BATTER RECIPES, WITH A FEW EXTRA FOR CHOICE.

THESE BATTERS WILL BE USED THROUGHOUT WITH OTHER MEATS AND DISHES

F I S H - B A S I C B A T T E R

Ingredients:

- 120g/ 1 cup plain/all-purpose flour
- 900g/2lb cod/haddock or other white fish fillets (serves four)
- 2 tsp baking powder
- 1/2 tsp sea salt
- 250ml/1 cup cold water

Instructions:

1. Combine the flour, baking powder, and salt in a large mixing bowl, creating a depression in the centre. Add the water and mix until a smooth batter forms.
2. Use a deep frying method of choice. Preheat the oil to 180C/370F. While preheating, use kitchen roll/towel to dry the fillets thoroughly.
3. Coat the fillets in the wet batter before carefully lowering them into the heated oil/fat. Cook until they turn a delightful golden or darker brown. Let the fried fish drain on a rack and serve while still warm.

FISH - CIDER BATTER

Ingredients:

- 120g/1 cup self-raising/self-rising flour
- 900g/2lb cod/haddock or other white fish fillets (serves four)
- 1/4 tsp sea salt
- 1/4 tsp ground black pepper
- 250ml/1 cup of dry apple cider

Instructions:

1. Combine flour, salt and pepper in a mixing bowl and blend them using a fork. Gradually pour in the cider, stirring continuously with a whisk and scraping the bowl's edges until the batter reaches a smooth, thin batter. Add more cider if it is too thick. Cover the bowl and refridgerate for 30 minutes.
2. Use a deep frying method of choice. Preheat the oil/fat to 180C/370F. While preheating, use kitchen roll/towel to dry the fillets thoroughly.
3. Coat the fillets in the wet batter before carefully lowering them into the heated oil/fat. Cook until they turn a delightful golden or darker brown. Let the fried fish drain on a rack and serve while still warm.

FISH - DARK BEER BATTER

Ingredients:

- 120g/1 cup plain/all-purpose flour
- 900g/2lb cod/haddock or other white fish fillets (serves four)
- 250ml/1 cup dark beer
- 60g/ 1/2 cup cornflour/cornstarch
- 1/2 tsp baking powder
- 1/2 tsp sea salt
- 1/2 tsp ground black pepper
- Plain/all-purpose flour for dredging

Instructions:

1. Combine flour, cornflour/cornstarch and baking powder in a mixing bowl and blend them using a fork. Gradually pour in the beer, stirring continuously with a whisk and scraping the bowl's edges. Add beer until the batter reaches a smooth, thin batter. Add more water if it is too thick. Chill the batter in the fridge for one hour.
2. Use a deep frying method of choice. Preheat the oil/fat to 180C/370F. While preheating, use kitchen roll/towel to dry the fillets thoroughly before seasoning with salt and pepper.
3. Individually dredge each fillet in flour, then in the wet batter before carefully lowering them into the heated oil/fat. Cook until they turn a delightful golden or darker brown. Let the fried fish drain on a rack and serve while still warm.

FISH - EGG WHITES BATTER

Ingredients:

- 90g/ 3/4 cup self-raising/self-rising flour
- 70g/ 1/2 cup rice flour
- 60ml/ 1/4 cup olive oil
- 250ml/1 cup cold water
- 900g/2lb cod/haddock or other white fish fillets (serves four)
- 2 egg whites
- 1/4 tsp sea salt

Instructions:

1. Place the flour, rice flour and salt into a large mixing bowl. Create a depression in the centre and pour in the oil and water. Stir these ingredients until the mixture reaches a smooth, batter-like texture. Add more water if too thick.
2. In a different bowl, beat the egg white until it forms soft peaks. Gently fold this into the batter, ensuring it's evenly mixed. It's acceptable for there to be small lumps or streaks of egg white.
3. Use a deep frying method of choice. Preheat the oil/fat to 180C/370F. While preheating, use kitchen roll/towel to dry the fillets thoroughly.
4. Coat the fillets in the wet batter before carefully lowering them into the heated oil/fat. Cook until they turn a delightful golden or darker brown. Let the fried fish drain on a rack and serve while still warm.

F I S H - G A R L I C M A Y O -
B R E A D E D

Ingredients:

- 900g/2lb
  plaice/flounder/dab/turbot/ or other
  flat fish, or other white fish fillets
  (serves four)
- 200g/2 cups of fine white
  breadcrumbs
- 3 garlic cloves, finely grated/minced
- 1 tbsp fresh parsley, finely chopped
- 1/4 tsp sea salt
- 1/4 tsp ground black pepper
- 30ml/2 tbsp butter, melted
- 60ml/ 1/4 cup mayonnaise
- 2 tbsp olive oil

Instructions:

1. In a shallow bowl, mix breadcrumbs, parsley, garlic, melted butter, olive
   oil, salt, and black pepper until well combined.
2. Use kitchen roll/towel to dry the fish thoroughly.
3. Apply a thin layer of mayonnaise to all sides of each fillet, then firmly
   press them into the breadcrumb mixture, ensuring a thorough coating.
4. Use a deep frying method of choice. Heat the oil/fat to 180C/370F.
5. Carefully lower the coated fish into the heated oil/fat. Cook until golden
   brown. Let the fried fish drain on a rack and serve while still warm.

F I S H - G L U T E N - F R E E B A T T E R

Ingredients:

- 120g/1 cup rice flour
- 900g/2lb cod/haddock or other white fish fillets (serves four)
- 1 tbsp baking powder
- 1/4 tsp sea salt
- 1/4 tsp ground black pepper
- 30g/4 tbsp cornflour/cornstarch
- 180ml/ 3/4 cup cold water

Instructions:

1. Combine flour, cornflour/cornstarch and baking powder in a mixing bowl and blend them using a fork. Gradually pour in the cold water, stirring continuously with a whisk and scraping the bowl's edges until the batter reaches a smooth, thin batter. Add more water if it is too thick.
2. Use a deep frying method of choice. Preheat the oil/fat to 180C/370F. While preheating, use kitchen roll/towel to dry the fillets thoroughly before seasoning with salt and pepper.
3. Coat the fillets in the wet batter before carefully lowering them into the heated oil/fat. Cook until they turn a delightful golden or darker brown. Let the fried fish drain on a rack and serve while still warm.

FISH - LAGER BATTER

Ingredients:

- 120g/1 cup plain/all-purpose flour
- 900g/2lb cod/haddock or other white fish fillets (serves four)
- 1 tsp paprika
- 1/2 tsp sea salt
- 1/2 tsp ground black pepper
- 1 tsp garlic powder or 2 grated cloves
- 1 lightly beaten egg
- 250ml/1 cup lager of choice
- Plain/all-purpose flour for dredging

Instructions:

1. Combine 120g/1 cup of flour, garlic, and paprika in a large bowl. Incorporate a lightly whisked egg, then slowly add the cold lager, whisking continuously until the batter is smooth and free of clumps. Add more water if it is too thick.
2. Use a deep frying method of choice. Preheat the oil/fat to 180C/370F.
3. While preheating, use kitchen roll/towel to dry the fillets thoroughly before seasoning with salt and pepper.
4. Individually dredge each fillet in flour, then in the wet batter before carefully lowering them into the heated oil/fat. Cook until they turn a delightful golden or darker brown. Let the fried fish drain on a rack and serve while still warm.

MALT VINEGAR BATTER

Ingredients:

- 120g/ 1 cup plain/all-purpose flour
- 900g/2lb cod/haddock or other white fish fillets (serves four)
- 60g/ 1/2 cup cornflour/cornstarch
- 1 tsp baking powder
- 80ml/ 1/3 cup malt vinegar
- 30 ml/ 2 tbsp soda/sparking water
- 1/4 tsp sea salt

Instructions:

1. Combine the flour, cornflour/cornstarch, baking powder, and salt in a large bowl. Slowly add the vinegar and soda/sparkling water, whisking continuously until you achieve a smooth batter. Allow the batter to sit for 15 minutes.
2. Use a deep-frying method of choice. Heat the oil/fat to 180C/370F. While preheating, use kitchen roll/towel to dry the fillets thoroughly. Coat the fish in the batter, letting any excess drip off.
3. Carefully lower the coated fish into the heated oil/fat. Cook until they turn a delightful golden or darker brown. Let the fried fish drain on a rack and serve while still warm.

FISH - MILK BATTER

Ingredients:

- 120g/ 1 cup plain/all-purpose flour
- 900g/2lb cod/haddock or other white fish fillets (serves four)
- 125ml/ 1/2 cup milk
- 1/4 tsp sea salt
- 1/4 tsp ground black pepper
- 125ml/ 1/2 cup cold water

Instructions:

1. Combine the flour, baking powder, salt and pepper in a large bowl. Gently mix in cold water and milk and beat into a smooth batter.
2. Use a deep frying method of choice. Preheat the oil to 180C/370F. While preheating, use kitchen roll/towel to dry the fillets thoroughly. Coat the fish in the batter, letting any excess drip off a little.
3. Carefully lower the coated fish into the heated oil/fat. Cook until they turn a delightful golden or darker brown. Let the fried fish drain on a rack and serve while still warm.

F I S H - P A N K O - B R E A D E D

Ingredients:

- 60g/ 1/2 cup plain/all-purpose flour
- 900g/2lb
  plaice/flounder/dab/turbot/ or other
  flat fish, or other white fish fillets
  (serves four)
- 200g/2 cups of Panko breadcrumbs
- 1/4 tsp sea salt
- 2 eggs, beaten

Instructions:

1. In a shallow dish, combine the flour, salt, and eggs. Use another dish for the Panko breadcrumbs. Use kitchen roll/towel to dry the fillets thoroughly.
2. First, coat the fish fillets in the flour and egg mixture, then in the Panko, ensuring the breadcrumbs adhere well to each side.
3. Use a deep frying method of choice. Heat the oil/fat to 180C/370F.
4. Carefully lower the coated fish into the heated oil/fat. Cook until they turn a delightful golden brown. Let the fried fish drain on a rack and serve while still warm.

FISH - PARMESAN - BREADED

Ingredients:

- 900g/2 lb
  plaice/flounder/dab/turbot/ or other
  flat fish, or other white fish fillets
  (serves four)
- 200g/2 cups of Panko breadcrumbs
- 1 tsp paprika
- 2 eggs, beaten
- 45g/ 1/3 cup Parmesan,
  grated/shredded
- 1 tbsp fresh parsley, finely chopped

Instructions:

1. Combine breadcrumbs, cheese, parsley, and paprika in a shallow dish. Use kitchen roll/towel to dry the fish thoroughly.
2. Coat the fish first in the beaten egg whites, followed by the breadcrumb mixture. Refridgerate the fish in a single layer for 1 hour.
3. Use a deep frying method of choice. Heat the oil/fat to 180C/370F.
4. Carefully lower the coated fish into the heated oil/fat. Cook until they turn golden brown. Let the fried fish drain on a rack and serve while still warm.

FISH - SODA/SPARKLING WATER BATTER

Ingredients:

- 120g/1 cup plain/all-purpose flour
- 60g/ 1/2 cup of flour for dredging
- 900g/2lb cod/haddock or other white fish fillets (serves four)
- 1/2 cup cornflour/cornstarch
- 1/4 tsp sea salt
- 1/4 tsp ground black pepper
- 2 tsp baking powder
- 250ml/1 cup cold sparkling or soda water

Instructions:

1. Combine 120g/1 cup of flour, cornflour/cornstarch, baking powder, salt, and pepper in a bowl. Gently mix in cold soda water until just blended with the dry ingredients, ensuring not to overmix; a few lumps are acceptable. The batter should have a thin consistency that easily drips off a spoon. Add more soda water if the batter seems too thick.
2. Use a deep frying method of choice. Preheat the oil to 180C/370F. While preheating, use kitchen roll/towel to dry the fillets thoroughly. Coat the fish lightly in the flour for dredging in a shallow bowl, dripping off any excess, before immersing it in the batter.
3. Carefully lower the coated fish into the heated oil/fat. Cook until they turn a delightful golden or darker brown. Let the fried fish drain on a rack and serve while still warm.

FISH - SOUTHERN FRIED BATTER

Ingredients:

- 120g/ 1 cup plain/all-purpose flour
- 900g/2lb cod/haddock or other white fish fillets (serves four)
- 250ml/1 cup buttermilk
- 1 tsp baking powder
- 1/4 tsp sea salt
- 1/4 tsp ground black pepper
- 60g/ 1/2 cup cornmeal (white)
- 2 tsp Old Bay Seasoning
- 2 eggs beaten

Instructions:

1. In a bowl, whisk the eggs into the buttermilk until well combined. Use kitchen roll or a towel to dry the fillets thoroughly before seasoning with salt and pepper. Submerge the fish in this mixture and let it marinate for 15 minutes.
2. Combine the flour, cornmeal, and Old Bay Seasoning in a different bowl. After marinating, lift the fish from the buttermilk blend and carefully coat all sides in the flour mixture. Place the coated fish on a baking tray and let it sit for 5 minutes.
3. Use a deep frying method of choice. Preheat the oil/fat to 180C/370F. Carefully lower the coated fish into the heated oil/fat. Cook until they turn a delightful golden or darker brown. Let the fried fish drain on a rack and serve while still warm.

FISH - TEMPURA BATTER

Ingredients:

- 120g/ 1 cup plain/all-purpose flour
- 70g/ 1/2 cup cornflour/cornstarch
- 900g/2lb cod/haddock or other white fish fillets (serves four) Cut into smaller pieces about 5cm/2 inches
- 1 tsp baking soda
- 1 tsp baking powder
- 1/2 tsp granulated sugar
- 250ml/1 cup very cold water
- 1 egg

Instructions:

1. Combine the flour, cornflour/cornstarch, baking soda, baking powder, and sugar in a large mixing bowl and create a depression in the centre.
2. In a different bowl, beat the egg and whisk in the cold water, then slowly add this mixture to the flour mixture, mixing until as smooth or as fairly smooth.
3. Use a deep frying method of choice. Preheat the oil/fat to 180C/370F. While preheating, use kitchen roll/towel to dry the fillets thoroughly.
4. Coat the fillets in the wet batter before carefully lowering them into the heated oil/fat. Cook until they turn a delightful golden or darker brown. Let the fried fish drain on a rack and serve while still warm.

COD ROE - BATTERED

Ingredients:

- Choose one of the batters created for the fish, and choose a light batter, like soda/sparkling water, vinegar, or tempura
- 2 tins/cans pressed cod roe, about 200g/7 oz per tin/can
- 60g/ 1/2 cup plain/all-purpose flour for dredging

Instructions:

1. Prepare the batter.
2. Carefully remove the roe from the tins/cans and slice into desired thicknesses. Ideally, two tins/cans would make four battered cod roe.
3. Use a deep-frying method of your choice. Heat the oil/fat to 180C/370F.
4. Dredge the slices in flour, then coat them in the batter and carefully lower them into the hot oil/fat.
5. Remove them once they turn golden brown.
6. Let them drain on a rack and serve while still warm.

CRAB CAKES

Ingredients:

- 450g/1 lb crab meat, tinned/canned or fresh
- 1/2 onion, peeled, finely chopped
- 1 tbsp butter, softened
- 2 tbsp fresh parsley, finely chopped
- 1/4 tsp sea salt
- 1/4 tsp ground black pepper
- 2 tbsp plain/all-purpose flour
- 60g/ 1/2 cup of plain/all-purpose flour for dredging
- 100g/1 cup fine white breadcrumbs
- 4 eggs
- 1 tsp Worcestershire sauce

Instructions:

1. Combine the crab meat with the rest of the ingredients except for the breadcrumbs and 2 eggs. Shape the mixture in the crab cake sizes about 10 cm/4 inches across and about 2.5 cm/1 inch thick, then place them in the fridge for 1 hour.
2. Prepare three bowls—one with dredging flour, another with two beaten eggs, and the third with breadcrumbs. Coat a crab cake in the flour, then the eggs, and finally, the breadcrumbs. Continue with the rest of the crab cakes.
3. Use a deep frying method of choice. Heat the oil/fat to 180C/370F. Gently lower the crab cakes in and cook until they turn a delightful golden or darker brown and are cooked through. Let the crab cakes drain on a rack and serve while still warm.

CRAB/FISH STICKS - BATTER

Ingredients:

- Batter. Choose a light batter from the battered fish recipes, such as the tempura or soda/sparkling water batter
- 60g/ 1/2 cup plain/all-purpose flour for dredging
- 1 pack of crab/fish sticks, often 16, or anywhere between 10 and 20

Instructions:

1. Create the batter.
2. Use a deep frying method of choice. Preheat the oil/fat to 180C/370F.
3. While preheating, use a kitchen roll/towel to thoroughly dry the crab/fish sticks.
4. Individually dredge each crab/fish stick in flour and then in the wet batter before carefully lowering them into the heated oil/fat. Cook until they turn a delightful golden or darker brown. Let them drain on a rack and serve while still warm.

FISH CAKES - BATTERED

Ingredients:

- Choose one of the batters created for the fish, and choose a heavy batter, like beer, but not soda/sparkling water, vinegar, or tempura
- 450g/1lb cod/haddock or other white fish fillets (serves four)
- 5 medium potatoes, peeled
- 1/2 tsp ground black pepper
- 1/4 tsp sea salt
- 1 tsp dried parsley
- 1 tsp dried thyme
- 4 spring onions, finely chopped
- 1 tbsp butter
- 60g/ 1/2 cup of plain/all-purpose flour for dredging

Instructions:

1. Peel and boil the potatoes. While the potatoes are cooking, finely chop your choice of fish and place it in a large bowl with the chopped spring onions.
2. Create the batter.
3. Once the potatoes are boiled, mash them, incorporating butter. Combine the mashed potatoes with the chopped fish and spring onions, then add the thyme, parsley, salt, and pepper.
4. Dust a work surface with flour. Take a handful of the mixture, roll it, and pat it into a circular, flat shape about 2.5 cm/1 inch thick and up to 10 cm/4 inches in diameter.
5. Use a deep frying method of choice. Heat the oil/fat to 180C/370F.
6. Dredge the fish cakes in the flour, then coat them in the batter. Carefully lower them into the hot oil/fat. Remove them once they turn a dark golden brown, ensuring the fish is cooked. After frying, let them drain on a rack and serve while warm.

FISH FINGERS - JUMBO - BATTERED

Ingredients:

- Choose one of the batters created for the fish
- 900g/2 lb cod/haddock or other large white fish fillets, of a depth of about 13mm/ 1/2 inch thick, sliced into lengths of about 15 cm/6 inches and about 2.5 cm/1 inch wide
- Enough wooden skewers to go through the slices of fish lengthways
- 1/2 tsp ground black pepper
- 1/4 tsp sea salt
- 60g/ 1/2 cup of flour for dredging

Instructions:

1. Create the batter.
2. Thread each skewer through each strip of fish lengthways. This will stop the fish from breaking during coating and cooking. Cook any leftover pieces of fish that are not quite uniform or large.
3. Use a deep frying method of choice. Heat the oil/fat to 180C/370F.
4. Dredge the skewered fish in the flour, then in the batter. Carefully lower the coated fish into the heated oil/fat. Cook until they turn golden brown. Let the jumbo fish fingers drain on a rack and serve while still warm.

SCALLOPS - BREADED

Ingredients:

- Choose one of the batters created for the fish, and choose a light batter, like soda/sparkling water, vinegar, or tempura
- 450g/1 lb scallops, fresh or defrosted
- 60g/ 1/2 cup of plain/all-purpose flour for dredging
- 2 eggs, beaten

Instructions:

1. Prepare the batter
2. Thoroughly dry the scallops with kitchen roll/towel.
3. Use a deep-frying method of your choice. Heat the oil/fat to 180C/370F.
4. Dredge the precooked sausages in the dredging flour.
5. Coat them in the batter, and carefully lower them into the hot oil/fat.
6. Remove them once they turn golden brown.

SCAMPI - BREADED

Ingredients:

- 450g/1 lb large raw langoustines, peeled, deveined. As the work scampi referred to peeled prawn tails, you might also use prawns for this if langoustines are unavailable
- 1/4 tsp sea salt
- 1/4 tsp ground black pepper
- 2 eggs, beaten
- 120g/1 cup plain/all-purpose flour
- 100g/1 cup fine white breadcrumbs

Instructions:

1. Season the peeled tails with salt and pepper. In a shallow dish, place the beaten egg.
2. Use a deep frying method of choice. Heat the oil/fat to 180C/370F.
3. Mix the breadcrumbs and flour in a separate shallow dish. Dip each tail into the egg mixture, then coat it evenly with the breadcrumb-flour mixture.
4. Carefully lower them into the hot oil/fat. Remove them once they turn golden, as the tails take little time to cook.

SQUID (CALAMARI) RINGS - BATTERED

Ingredients:

- Choose one of the batters created for the fish, and choose a light batter, like soda/sparkling water, vinegar, or tempura
- 450g/1 lb of prepared squid, which you can either slice yourself, have the fishmonger slice them, or buy squid rings
- 60g/ 1/2 cup plain/all-purpose flour for dredging.

Instructions:

1. Cut the squid tubes into rings approximately 13mm/ 1/2 inch thick. If there are any tentacles, keep them together, minus the head and beak.
2. Use a deep frying method of choice. Heat the oil/fat to 180C/370F.
3. Dredge the rings and any gangs of tentacles in the flour, then coat them in the batter.
4. Carefully lower them into the hot oil/fat. Remove them once they turn a light golden, which could be as soon as a minute or two, as the squid takes little time to cook. After frying, drain them on a rack and serve while still warm.

WHITEBAIT - BATTERED

Ingredients:

- Choose one of the batters created for the fish, and choose a light batter, like soda/sparkling water, vinegar, or tempura
- 450g/1 lb fresh whole whitebait
- 60g/ 1/2 cup plain/all-purpose flour for dredging

Instructions:

1. Prepare the batter.
2. Thoroughly dry the whitebait with kitchen roll/towel. If frozen, thaw the whitebait and dry them with kitchen roll/towel.
3. Use a deep-frying method of your choice. Heat the oil/fat to 180C/370F.
4. Dredge the whitebait in flour, then coat them in the batter and carefully lower them into the hot oil/fat, ideally in a frying basket, cooking them until they turn golden brown.
5. Remove them once they turn golden brown.
6. Let them drain on a rack and serve while still warm.

YORKSHIRE FISH CAKE

Ingredients:

- Choose one of the batters created for the fish, opting for a heavy batter, such as beer, rather than soda/sparkling water, vinegar, or tempura
- 8 large potatoes, peeled, sliced, about 5mm/ 1/5 inch thick
- White fish fillet, quite thin at about 1 cm/ 2/5 inch thick, and enough for a single layer the size of the sliced potato
- 60g/ 1/2 cup plain/all-purpose flour for dredging

Instructions:

1. Prepare the batter.
2. If the slices of potato are about 5mm/ 1/5 inch thick, they will be fine raw. If any thicker, parboil the potato slices so they are slightly cooked but still hold firm.
3. Use a deep-frying method of your choice. Heat the oil/fat to 180C/370F.
4. Place a single layer of raw white fish on one of the potato slices and cover the fish with another potato slice.
5. Dredge the potato fish sandwich in the flour.
6. Coat them in the batter and carefully lower them into the hot oil/fat. Remove them once they turn golden brown or until the potato slices are tender but firm and the batter is dark and cooked.
7. Let them drain on a rack and serve while still warm.

BACON CHEESEBURGER - BATTERED

Ingredients:

- Choose one of the batters created for the fish, and choose a heavy batter, like beer, but not soda/sparkling water, vinegar, or tempura
- 4 burger buns
- 8 burger patties of choice
- 4 slices of cheese of choice, enough to cover the size of a burger patty
- 4 slices of bacon of choice
- Optional: Sliced tomato and onion
- Toothpicks or cocktail sticks

Instructions:

1. Prepare the batter.
2. Fry or grill the burger patties, bacon, and any optional ingredients.
3. Cover a cooked patty on one side of a burger bun with cheese and top it with another patty.
4. Then, add any optional ingredients to the second patty before placing the top of the burger bun. Press the cheeseburger together quite firmly.
5. Using toothpicks, cocktail sticks, or skewers, skewer through the cheeseburger at two different angles to secure it for frying.
6. Use a deep frying method of choice. Heat the oil/fat to 180C/370F.
7. Dredge the bacon cheeseburger in the batter. Carefully lower it into the hot oil/fat. Remove it once it turns a golden brown.
8. Let them drain on a rack and serve while still warm.

BEEF BURGERS - BATTERED

Ingredients:

- Choose one of the batters created for the fish, and choose a light batter, like soda/sparkling water, vinegar, or tempura, as these batters will allow the beef burger to cook to the middle
- 900g/2 lb standard or fatty minced/ground beef, not lean
- 1 onion, peeled, finely chopped
- 1/4 tsp sea salt
- 1/4 tsp ground black pepper
- 2 eggs, beaten
- 1/4 tsp garlic powder
- 1/2 tsp cayenne pepper
- 60g/ 1/2 cup plain/all-purpose flour for dredging

Instructions:

1. Combine the beef burger ingredients, leaving the batter and dredging flour until later. Place the beef burger mixture in a covered bowl in the fridge for 1 hour to allow the ingredient with egg to bind before flattening the mixture into as many beef burgers as you want, to the size you prefer, but keep the thickness of the burgers to around 1 cm/ 2/5 inch.
2. Place one beef burger on a circle of parchment paper, then add a circle on the top. Do this by stacking them before leaving them in the coldest part of the refrigerator overnight, but not in the freezer. Remove them from the fridge when you cook them, which will help them maintain their structure.
3. Use a deep frying method of choice. Heat the oil/fat to 180C/370F.
4. Create the batter.
5. Dredge the beef burgers in the flour, then coat them in the batter. Carefully lower them into the hot oil/fat. Remove them once they turn a golden brown.

BLACK PUDDING - BATTERED

Ingredients:

- Choose one of the batters created for the fish, opting for a heavy batter, such as beer, rather than soda/sparkling water, vinegar, or tempura
- 450g/1 lb black pudding, cut into sausage shapes or rounds about 13mm/ 1/2 inch thick
- 60g/ 1/2 cup plain/all-purpose flour for dredging

Instructions:

1. Create the batter.
2. Use a deep frying method of choice. Heat the oil/fat to 180C/370F.
3. Dredge the fritters in the flour, patting the flower on in a thin layer, then coat them in the batter. Carefully lower them into the hot oil/fat. Remove them once they turn golden brown.
4. Let them drain on a rack and serve while still warm.

CHICKEN GOUJONS - BATTER

Ingredients:

- Choose one of the batters created for the fish, ideally the Basic or Southern-Fried
- 50g/ 1/2 cup of Panko or coarse breadcrumbs
- 700g/1 1/2 lb chicken tenderloins (tenders), or use whole skinless chicken breasts cut into strips, lengthways 2.5 cm/1 inch thick
- 60g/ 1/2 cup plain/all-purpose flour for dredging

Instructions:

1. Create the batter, then gently stir in the breadcrumbs.
2. Use a deep frying method of choice. Heat the oil/fat to 180C/370F.
3. Dredge the goujons in the dredging flour, then the batter/breadcrumb mix.
4. Carefully lower the goujons into the heated oil/fat. Cook until they turn a dark golden brown. Let them drain on a rack and serve while still warm, or eat later when cool.

CHICKEN PARMO - PART ONE - CHICKEN BREASTS

Ingredients:

- 450g/1 lb chicken breast fillets, sliced width ways thinly (you can also use other meats, tenderising them first)
- 150g/1 1/4 cups plain/all-purpose flour
- 30 ml/2 tbsp milk
- 1 tsp smoked paprika
- 1/4 tsp ground black pepper
- 1/2 tsp onion powder
- 2 eggs, beaten
- 1 tsp garlic powder
- 1/4 tsp cayenne pepper
- 100g/1 cup of white breadcrumbs

Instructions:

1. Combine the flour, garlic powder, smoked paprika, cayenne pepper, onion powder, and pepper in a shallow bowl. In another bowl, combine milk and eggs. Place breadcrumbs in a third dish.
2. Use a deep frying method of choice. Heat the oil/fat to 180C/370F.
3. Dip chicken slices into the flour, beaten egg and milk mixture, and coat with breadcrumbs.
4. Carefully lower the breaded chicken or other choice of tenderised meat into the heated oil/fat. Fry for 3 to 4 minutes or until they turn a dark golden brown. Let them drain on a rack and serve while warm with the sauce in part two.

For best results when combining the breaded meat with the sauce, aim to cook the meat concurrently with preparing the sauce. This ensures that once both components are ready, you can efficiently layer a portion of the sauce over each piece of the cooked breaded meat. Then, top it off with a sprinkle of grated/shredded cheddar cheese. Briefly place it under the grill to melt the cheese. Serve immediately after the cheese has melted.

CHICKEN PARMO - PART TWO - BECHAMEL SAUCE

Ingredients:

- 30g/1 oz butter
- 250ml/1 cup
- Pinch of sea salt and black pepper
- 20g/2 tbsp plain/all-purpose flour
- 1/2 tsp ground nutmeg
- 90g/ 3/4 cup cheddar cheese, grated/shredded

Instructions:

1. Melt the butter in a saucepan over medium heat. Whisk in the flour for about 2 minutes. Gradually add the milk, whisking continuously until very thick and smooth. If not thick enough to stay on top of the breaded meat, add more flour and stir it well.
2. Increase heat to medium-high, bring to a low boil, then simmer on low for 5 minutes, stirring occasionally. Add nutmeg, salt, and pepper, and stir to combine. Adjust seasoning if desired.

The sauce can be refrigerated for up to 5 days.

For best results when combining the breaded meat with the sauce, aim to cook the meat concurrently with preparing the sauce. This ensures that once both components are ready, you can efficiently layer a portion of the sauce over each piece of the cooked breaded meat. Then, top it off with a sprinkle of grated/shredded cheddar cheese. Briefly place it under the grill to melt the cheese. Serve immediately after the cheese has melted.

FAGGOTS - BATTERED

Ingredients:

- Choose one of the batters created for the fish, and choose a heavy batter, like beer, but not soda/sparkling water, vinegar, or tempura
- 450g/1 lb lean minced/ground beef
- 100g/ 3 oz lamb liver, finely chopped
- 100g/ 3 oz streaky bacon, finely chopped
- 1 small onion, peeled, grated/shredded
- 2 garlic cloves, grated/shredded
- 1 tbsp fresh parsley, finely chopped
- 2 tsp fresh thyme, finely chopped
- 2 tsp fresh sage, finely chopped
- 50g/ 1/2 cup white breadcrumbs
- 10ml/2 tsp English mustard

Instructions:

1. Create the batter.
2. Combine all the faggots ingredients in a large bowl and shape the mixture into 12 golf-ball-sized balls.
3. Place them in a baking/roasting tray. Cover the tray with foil and bake them for 45 minutes at 160C/320F or until they are cooked and not burnt. Preheating the oven is not necessary.
4. Use a deep frying method of choice. Heat the oil/fat to 180C/370F.
5. Carefully lower the battered faggots into the heated oil/fat. Cook until they turn a dark golden brown. Let them drain on a rack and serve while warm. The faggots are already cooked, so it is only the batter that needs cooking and the faggots heating through.
6. Ideally, serve with gravy.

HAGGIS - BATTERED

Ingredients:

- Prepare the Haggis to the Haggis pourover recipe in this book
- Prepare any batter of choice from the recipes in this book
- 1 large egg, beaten

Instructions:

1. Follow the Haggis cooking instructions from the Haggis pour-over recipe in this book.
2. Once cooked, allow the haggis to cool before mixing in the beaten egg.
3. Shape the haggis mixture into thick burger patty shapes. Refrigerate the haggis patties overnight.
4. Prepare the batter.
5. Use a deep-frying method of your choice. Heat the oil/fat to 180C/370F.
6. Coat them in the batter and carefully lower them into the hot oil/fat.
7. Remove them once they turn golden brown.
8. Let them drain on a rack and serve while still warm.

HAGGIS POUROVER

Ingredients for a basic chippy Haggis:

- 450g/ 1 lb minced/ground lamb
- 1 onion, peeled, finely chopped
- 225g/ 1/2 lb lamb liver, finely chopped
- 250ml/1 cup beef stock or broth
- 100g/ 3 1/2 oz pinhead oatmeal
- 1/2 tsp ground black pepper
- 1/4 tsp sea salt
- 1/2 tsp ground nutmeg
- 1/2 tsp ground coriander/cilantro seeds
- 1/2 tsp ground mace
- 1 tbsp butter

Instructions:

1. Preheat the oven to 175C/350F.
2. Melt the butter in a saucepan over medium heat. Add the onion and saute until soft, about 5 minutes.
3. Add the spices, seasonings, and softened onion, and cook for another 2 minutes. Add the minced/ground lamb and chopped chicken liver. Continue cooking to brown the meat.
4. Pour in the stock or broth, cover the saucepan, and let the mixture simmer for approximately 30 minutes.
5. Stir in the pinhead oatmeal and transfer the mixture to an ovenproof dish.
6. Cover the dish, place it in the oven, and bake for 30 minutes.
7. After this time, remove the cover and allow it to bake for 10 minutes to slightly crisp the top.
8. Cook chips to your liking or the recipes in this book, and pour over the Haggis mixture.

JOHN BULL

Ingredients:

- Choose one of the batters created for the fish, and choose a heavy batter, like beer, but not soda/sparkling water, vinegar, or tempura
- 450g/1lb minced/ground beef
- 5ml/1 tsp Worcestershire sauce
- 1 medium onion, peeled, finely chopped
- 1/4 tsp garlic powder
- 1 garlic clove, finely chopped
- Enough large potatoes to cut 6 large slices from them, no more than 5mm/ 1/5 inch thick. Thicker slices may require part boiling and drying so they are soft to bite after cooking
- 15ml/1 tbsp olive oil
- 60g/ 1/2 cup plain/all-purpose flour

Instructions:

1. Heat half the olive oil in a large frying pan/skillet over high heat. Fry onions and garlic until golden, then set them aside in a bowl.
2. Pour the remaining olive oil into the frying pan or skillet. Cook half of the beef mince in the pan. Once cooked, combine it with the sautéed onion, garlic, and Worcestershire sauce. Then, add the remaining mince and cook until all the mince is fully cooked. This method results in half of the mince being well done while the other half remains medium.
3. Create the batter.
4. Use a deep frying method of choice. Heat the oil/fat to 180C/370F.
5. Use a spoon to place a portion of the savoury mince onto one of the potato slices, shaping it to the edges. You can stack the mince to a thickness of about 1 cm/2/5 inch before covering it with another potato slice, effectively sandwiching the mince between the two slices. Press firmly on the top slice, ensuring the mince spreads to the edges. Trim off any excess mince with your finger to create a tidy sandwich.
6. Dredge the John Bull in the flour, then coat in the batter. Carefully lower it into the hot oil/fat. Remove it once it turns a golden brown.

L A M B   C H O P S   -
B A T T E R E D

Ingredients:

- Choose any of the batters created for the fish, ideally, the Parmesan cheese batter, which goes great with lamb
- 900g/2lb of lamb chops, ideally cutlet chops with long bones to handle and not too thick. Trim off any skin, but leave the fat on
- 60g/ 1/2 cup plain/all-purpose flour for dredging
- 30g/2 tbsp Parmesan cheese, grated/shredded

Instructions:

1. Create the batter.
2. Use kitchen roll/towel to dry any surface moisture from the chops.
3. Use a deep frying method of choice. Heat the oil/fat to 180C/370F.
4. Dredge the chops in the flour, then coat them in the batter. Carefully lower them into the hot oil/fat. Remove them once they turn a dark golden brown, ensuring the chops are cooked to your liking.

PIGS IN BLANKETS - BATTER

Ingredients:

- Choose one of the batters created for the fish, and choose a heavy batter, like beer, but not soda/sparkling water, vinegar, or tempura
- 10 to 20 cocktail sausages pre-cooked
- 5 to 10 rashers/slices of streaky bacon, cut in half lengthways
- Spray oil
- 10 to 20 cocktail sticks/toothpicks
- 60g/ 1/2 cup plain/all-purpose flour for dredging.

Instructions:

1. Create the batter.
2. Wrap a half slice of bacon around each sausage, using toothpicks or cocktail sticks to hold the bacon in place. Lightly spray each one with oil. Keep the sticks inserted while deep-frying, and only remove them after cooking. Dredge the pigs in blankets in the flour.
3. Use a deep frying method of choice. Heat the oil/fat to 180C/370F. Dip the pigs in blankets into the batter, then carefully lower them into the hot oil/fat. Fry until they turn golden. Since the cocktail sausages are already cooked, you're just cooking the batter, which should take only a few minutes. After frying, let them drain on a rack, remove the sticks, and serve while still warm.

RAG PUDDING

Ingredients:

- Create the pasty using the suet pastry recipe in this book (it should be enough to make 4 rag puddings)
- 450g/1 lb stewing steak chunks, not more than about 15mm/ 1/2 inch in size
- There is no beef kidney in this particular recipe, but feel free to add half a cup if you prefer
- 1/2 onion, peeled, finely chopped
- 2 tbsp cornflour/cornstarch
- 1/4 tsp sea salt
- 1/2 tsp ground black pepper
- 60ml/ 1/4 cup port
- 60 ml/ 1/4 cup of beef stock or broth
- 2 egg yolks, beaten

Instructions:

1. Prepare the suet pastry.
2. Brown the onion, stewing steak and optional kidney in a saucepan.
3. Stir in the stock or broth and port, as well as salt and pepper, allowing the mixture to simmer gently for an hour.
4. In a separate bowl, create a slurry by mixing cornflour/cornstarch with water. Stir it into the meat mixture to thicken it slightly. Continue cooking for an additional 10 minutes. Remove from heat and allow to cool.
5. Roll the dough into a large square or smaller individual squares for each guest on a floured surface.
6. Spread the cooled meat mixture on one half of the square or individual squares, then roll it up, sealing the edge with an egg yolk.
7. Wrap the roll or rolls in muslin, securing the ends with string to form a sausage-like shape.
8. Cook it/them in a large pot of simmering water (not boiling) for up to or over 2 hours or until the rag pudding pastry is tender.

S A U S A G E - B A T T E R E D

Ingredients:

- 240g/2 cups self-raising/self-rising flour
- 375ml/ 1 1/2 cups cold water
- 8 to 10 Large or Jumbo sausages
- 60g/ 1/2 cup of plain/all-purpose flour for dredging
- 1/2 tsp bicarbonate of soda
- 1 large egg

Instructions:

1. Precook the sausages and allow them to cool at room temperature.
2. Combine self-raising/self-rising flour and bicarbonate of soda in a large bowl.
3. Add the water and egg and whisk these together until you achieve a batter.
4. Use a deep-frying method of your choice. Heat the oil/fat to 180C/370F.
5. Dredge the precooked sausages in the dredging flour.
6. Coat them in the batter, and carefully lower them into the hot oil/fat.
7. Remove them once they turn golden brown.
8. Let them drain on a rack and serve while still warm.

S P A M - B A T T E R E D

Ingredients:

- Choose one of the batters created for the fish
- 1 tin/can of Spam, cut into 8 equal-thickness slices
- 60g/1 cup plain/all-purpose flour for dredging

Instructions:

1. Create the batter.
2. Use a deep frying method of choice. Heat the oil/fat to 180C/370F.
3. Dredge the fritters in the flour, then coat them in the batter. Carefully lower them into the hot oil/fat. Remove them once they turn golden brown.
4. Let them drain on a rack and serve while still warm.

S P A M   B A L L S

Ingredients:

- 1 tin/can of spam, diced to 5mm/ 1/5 inch chunks)
- 1 tsp baking powder
- 1/2 tsp ground black pepper
- 1/2 tsp onion powder
- 125ml/ 1/2 cup of milk
- 120g/1 cup plain/all-purpose flour
- 1/2 tsp sea salt
- 1/2 tsp garlic powder
- 1 egg, beaten

Instructions:

1. Whisk together flour, baking powder, salt, pepper, garlic powder, and onion powder in a large bowl. Add egg and milk to the mixture and stir until a thick batter forms. Add more flour if the batter is too thin to handle.
2. Mix in diced Spam and shape the batter into small rounds about the size of golf balls.
3. Use a deep frying method of choice. Heat the oil/fat to 180C/370F.
4. Carefully lower them into the hot oil/fat. Remove them once they turn a dark golden brown.
5. Let them drain on a rack and serve while still warm, or eat later when cool.

STEAK AND KIDNEY PUDDING

Ingredients:

- Create the pasty using the suet pastry recipe in this book (it should be enough to make 6 puddings)
- 15g/ 1/2 oz of butter
- 2 garlic cloves, grated/shredded
- 20g/ 2 tbsp plain/all-purpose flour
- 225g/8 oz ox/beef kidney
- 1 onion, peeled, finely chopped
- 15ml/1 tbsp Worcestershire sauce
- 125ml/ 1/2 cup of beef stock or broth
- 700g/1 1/2 lb braising steak or other lean steak

Instructions:

1. Prepare the suet pastry and roll it out thinly. Line 6 pudding tins, letting the pastry overhang slightly, and save some pastry for the lids. Grease the tins lightly with butter.
2. Remove all but the tender flesh from the kidneys, chop the tender flesh into 13mm/ 1/2 inch pieces, and place in a large bowl. Add similarly diced steak, onion, garlic, and flour. Mix well and fill the pastry-lined tins.
3. Mix Worcestershire sauce and stock, and pour over the meat in each tin.
4. Cover the mixture with pastry lids, sealing the edges.
5. Secure foil over each tin with string. Place a plate at the bottom of a large saucepan and stand the pudding tins on it.
6. Add water just below the tin lips, and bring it to just short of a boil. Reduce to a simmer and cook for 2+ hours or until pastry is tender.

S U E T   P A S T R Y

Ingredients:

- Enough to make 8 individual pork pies or 6 puddings, which can be filled with cooked meats and vegetables of your choice
- 240g/2 cups self-raising/self-rising flour
- 125g/4 oz grated/shredded suet, freshly prepared from raw suit from a butcher or pre-made in products like ATORA Shredded Beef Suet, found in most popular supermarkets
- 100ml/3 1/2 oz cold water
- 1/2 tsp fine sea salt

Instructions:

1. Combine the dry ingredients, then add the cold water until the mixture forms a stiff dough.
2. Refridgerate the dough for 30 minutes.
3. Transfer the dough onto a floured work surface and roll it to a 5mm/ 1/5 inch thickness.
4. Cut out shapes to accommodate the tins, trays or dishes you want to line and grease them with butter or oil before lining them with the suet dough.
5. Suet pastry can be steamed or baked and used with meat, savoury, or fruit fillings.

WIGAN KEBAB

Ingredients:

- 1 meat and potato pie. Ready cooked.
- 1 burger bun (bap, barmcake, etc.)
- Butter

Instructions:

1. Ideally, the meat and potato should be cooked and left to cool at room temperature, or they can be slightly warm from cooking.
2. Use a deep-frying method of your choice. Heat the oil/fat to 180C/370F.
3. Slice open the buns and butter each side.
4. Gently lower the meat and potato pie into the hot oil/fat and cook until the pie is heated through. (Alternatively, bake or air-fry the pie if you prefer).
5. Place the pie directly onto one half of the bun, then cover with the other half and serve.
6. Optionally, add a little gravy or mushy pea juice (pea wet) if desired.

CHEESE STICKS - BREADED

Ingredients:

- 2 beaten eggs
- 60g/ 1/2 cup plain/all-purpose flour
- 100g/1 cup fine white breadcrumbs
- 1/2 tsp garlic powder
- 10 to 15 mozzarella/cheese sticks
- 1/2 tsp Italian seasoning
- 1/4 tsp sea salt
- 1/4 tsp ground black pepper
- 60g/2 oz Parmesan cheese, grated/shredded

Instructions:

1. Place flour in a shallow bowl and beaten eggs in another. Combine breadcrumbs, garlic powder, Italian seasoning, salt, pepper, and Parmesan in a third shallow bowl.
2. Dredge each cheese in the flour, then the eggs and breadcrumb mixture, coating thoroughly.
3. Use a deep frying method of choice. Heat the oil/fat to 180C/370F. Gently lower the cheese sticks in and cook until they turn a delightful golden or darker brown and are cooked through. Let them drain on a rack and serve while still warm.

CHIP BUTTY - BATTERED

Ingredients:

- Choose one of the batters created for the fish, and choose a heavy batter, like beer, but not soda/sparkling water, vinegar, or tempura.
- One small portion of chippy chips or the equivalent of chips cooked at home
- As many bread rolls/baps/barms, or whatever you like to call them, as is required for the number of people

Instructions:

1. Create the batter.
2. Open the bread and neatly arrange the chips in two tight rows, one on top of the other, to ensure they are snugly packed. Press down on both sides of the bread to compress the chips, creating a compact and firm sandwich.
3. If you have scratchings, mushy peas, gravy, or curry available, consider spooning a tablespoon of each onto the initial layer of chips. Then, proceed to add the second layer. Be cautious not to add too much; excessive filling may overflow when pressing the bread together.
4. Use a deep-frying method of choice. Heat the oil/fat to 180C/370F. Gently coat each chip butty in the batter, then carefully lower it into the hot oil/fat. Fry it until it's golden.
5. Since all the ingredients inside the butty are already cooked, you only need to ensure the batter is fully cooked. Monitor the frying process closely, waiting for the batter to turn golden and crisp.

HALLOUMI - BATTERED

Ingredients:

- Choose one of the batters created for the fish, and choose a light batter, like soda/sparkling water, vinegar, or tempura
- 225g/8 oz halloumi, sliced into sticks or odd shapes about 2.5cm/1 inch thick

Instructions:

1. Prepare the batter.
2. Thoroughly remove the surface moisture from the halloumi sticks with a kitchen roll/towel.
3. Use a deep-frying method of your choice. Heat the oil/fat to 180C/370F.
4. Coat the sticks in the batter and carefully lower them into the hot oil/fat.
5. Remove them once they turn golden brown.
6. Let them drain on a rack and serve while still warm.

MINTED MUSHY PEAS

Ingredients:

- 2 garlic cloves, grated/shredded
- 450g/1 lb dried marrowfat peas
- 1/2 tsp dried mint or 1 tbsp fresh mint, finely chopped
- Pinch of sea salt and ground black pepper
- 2 tsp baking soda

Instructions:

1. Combine the dried peas, baking soda, and mint in a heatproof bowl. Pour boiling water over these ingredients to cover them completely. Allow the mixture to soak overnight.
2. The following day, drain the peas, but keep a glass of the soaking water to one side.
3. Place the drained peas, garlic, pepper, and salt in a food processor. Start blending the ingredients, gradually adding the water you saved until the mixture achieves the desired consistency.
4. When you're ready to eat, heat the blended pea mixture.

MUSHROOMS - BREADED

Ingredients:

- 120g/1 cup plain/all-purpose flour
- 450g/1 lb button, or slightly larger mushroom with stalks left in
- 1/4 tsp sea salt
- 1/4 tsp ground black pepper
- 1 tsp baking powder
- 250ml/1 cup cold water
- 60g/ 1/2 cup cornflour/cornstarch
- 200g/2 cups of Panko, or other coarse breadcrumbs

Instructions:

1. Combine flour, cornflour/cornstarch, baking powder, salt and pepper in a mixing bowl. Gradually add the cold water to create a smooth batter.
2. Use a deep frying method of choice. Heat the oil/fat to 180C/370F.
3. Dip the mushrooms into the batter, allowing any excess to drip off, then pat the breadcrumbs lightly onto the batter on the mushrooms, ensuring an even coating.
4. Carefully lower the coated mushroom into the heated oil/fat. Cook until they turn a golden brown. Serve while still warm.

ONION RINGS - BATTERED

Ingredients:

- 1 large onion, peeled and sliced into thick rings
- 60g/ 1/2 cup plain/all-purpose flour
- 1/2 tsp sea salt
- 1/2 tsp paprika
- 60g/ 1/2 cup cornflour/cornstarch
- 1/2 tsp garlic powder
- Spray oil

Instructions:

1. Combine the flour, cornflour, salt, garlic powder and paprika in a large bowl.
2. Spray a little oil on the onion rings and dip them into the flour mixture.
3. Use a deep frying method of choice. Heat the oil/fat to 180C/370F. Gently lower them into the hot oil/fat. Fry them until they achieve a golden colour.
4. Remove them and spread them out on kitchen roll or towel for a few seconds to remove excess oil or fat.

ORANGE CHIPS

Ingredients:

- 120g/1 cup plain/all-purpose flour
- 1/2 tsp paprika
- 1 tsp baking powder
- 125ml/ 1/2 cup cold milk
- 125ml/ 1/2 cup cold water
- 4 large potatoes, peeled, chipped
- 60g/ 1/2 cup plain/all-purpose flour for dredging

Instructions:

1. Wash and thoroughly dry the chipped potatoes.
2. Blend the 120g/ 1 cup of flour with the paprika and baking powder in a large mixing bowl.
3. Gradually incorporate the milk and water, continuously whisking to achieve a smooth consistency.
4. Add a few drops of orange food colouring to the mix (optional).
5. Use a deep-frying method of your choice. Heat the oil/fat to 180C/370F.
6. Dredge the chips in the dredging flour, coat them in the batter, and carefully lower them into the hot oil/fat. A chip basket could be helpful.
7. Remove them once they turn golden brown, and the chips cave in easily under light pressure.
8. Let them drain on a rack and serve while still warm.

OREOS - BATTERED

Ingredients:

- 1 packet of Oreos
- 200g/7 oz pancake mixture
- 250g/1 cup milk
- 1 egg, beaten
- 4 drops vanilla extract
- 1 tsp olive oil
- 1 tbsp icing/powdered sugar or plain/all-purpose flour for dusting

Instructions:

1. Arrange the fish on a baking tray lined with kitchen paper and dab thoroughly to remove excess moisture.
2. Whisk the oil, egg, vanilla extract, and milk in a large bowl. Then, fold in the pancake mix, stirring until smooth and free from lumps.
3. Use a deep-frying method of your choice. Heat the oil/fat to 180C/370F.
4. Coat the Oreos in the batter, carefully lower them into the hot oil/fat, and cook until golden brown.
5. Dust them with icing sugar or flour prior to serving.

PEA FRITTER

Ingredients:

- Use my minted mushy peas recipe to create the mushy peas needed for this recipe
- Choose one of the batters created for the fish, and choose a light batter, like soda/sparkling water, vinegar, or tempura
- 60g/ 1/2 cup plain/all-purpose flour for dredging

Instructions:

1. Prepare the mushy peas according to my recipe.
2. Ensure the mushy peas are cool before placing them in a dish in the fridge for about an hour.
3. Remove the firm mushy peas from the fridge, shape them into balls about 5 cm/2 inches in diameter, and flatten them slightly with the palm of your hand to prevent them from rolling around.
4. Place them apart on a tray lined with parchment paper and place them in the freezer overnight or for at least 2 hours. When ready to cook them, let them partly thaw so they are still very firm but not frozen to the core.
5. Use a deep-frying method of your choice. Heat the oil/fat to 180C/370F.
6. Dredge the frozen mushy pea patties in flour, then coat them in the batter and carefully lower them into the hot oil/fat.
7. Remove them once they turn golden brown, and a toothpick goes through easily and comes out hot.
8. Let them drain on a rack and serve while still warm.

PICKLED ONIONS - BREADED

Ingredients:

- 60g/ 1/2 cup plain/all-purpose flour
- Large pickled onions, 6 per person
- 2 tsp toasted sesame seeds
- 1 or 2 beaten eggs, depending on the quantity of pickled onions
- 100g/1 cup of fine white breadcrumbs

Instructions:

1. In a bowl, add the flour; in another bowl, add the breadcrumbs; and in a third bowl, add the beaten eggs.
2. Use a deep frying method of choice. Heat the oil/fat to 180C/370F.
3. Shake off excess vinegar from the pickles, roll them in the flour, then the egg, then the breadcrumbs, then gently lower them into the hot oil/fat.
4. The pickles are ready when the batter is cooked; they do not need much time, so keep an eye on them.

PIZZA CALZONE - BATTERED

Ingredients:

- Choose one of the batters created for the fish, and choose a heavy batter, like beer, but not soda/sparkling water, vinegar, or tempura.
- 1 pre-made individual-sized pizza to fit the deep-fryer

Alternatively

- 1 pre-made individual-sized pizza base
- 30ml/2 tbsp pizza sauce
- 80g/ 3 oz cheddar cheese, grated/shredded
- 60g/ 1/2 cup mozzarella, grated/shredded

Instructions:

1. Create the batter.
2. Warm the pizza base in a microwave for 20 seconds to make it flexible enough to bend without breaking. Then, evenly spread pizza sauce on the base and top it with mozzarella and cheddar cheese. Fold the base in half to form the calzone, pressing the edges together tightly to securely encapsulate the sauce and cheese.
3. If using a pre-made cheese and tomato pizza, briefly microwave it for a few seconds until it's pliable enough to fold in half without cracking.
4. Use a deep-frying method of choice. Heat the oil/fat to 180C/370F. Gently coat the calzones in batter, then carefully lower them into the hot oil/fat. Fry them until they achieve a golden colour.

POTATO SCALLOP (DAB)

Ingredients:

- Choose one of the batters created for the fish, opting for a heavy batter, such as beer, rather than soda/sparkling water, vinegar, or tempura

- 2 to 3 large potatoes, peeled and sliced to about 5mm (1/5 inch) thick. If the slices are any thicker, they may need to be parboiled to soften them slightly
- 60g/ 1/2 cup plain/all-purpose flour for dredging

Instructions:

1. Prepare the batter.
2. Use a deep frying method of choice. Heat the oil/fat to 180C/370F.
3. Dredge the potato slices in the flour for a thorough coating, then tap off the excess.
4. Coat them in the batter and carefully lower them into the hot oil/fat. Remove them once they turn golden brown.
5. Let them drain on a rack and serve while still warm.

SALT AND PEPPER CHIPS

Ingredients:

- Once this recipe's ingredients are prepared but not cooked, set it aside and cook the chips to one of our chips recipes.
- 1 green bell pepper, deseeded, diced
- 1 green chilli pepper, deseeded, diced
- 1 onion, peeled, diced
- 1 tsp garlic powder
- 4 spring onions, chopped
- 1 tsp onion powder
- 1/2 tsp Chinese Five Spice powder
- 1 tsp Szechuan peppercorns, crushed
- 15ml/1 tbsp sesame oil
- 15ml/1 tbsp sweet chilli sauce
- Fresh coriander/cilantro, chopped

Instructions:

1. Mix diced onion, red and green chilli peppers, and bell pepper in a large bowl. Thoroughly incorporate garlic powder, onion powder, Szechuan pepper, Chinese Five Spice, salt, and sesame oil into the vegetables. Let this mixture sit aside until the chips are ready.
2. After frying, place the chips on paper towels to remove excess oil. Next, saute the pepper and onion mixture in a large wok or frying pan/skillet until the vegetables are soft yet still hold their shape.
3. Incorporate the cooked chips into the sauteed vegetables, adding any remaining ingredients except fresh coriander/cilantro, spring onion, and sweet chilli sauce. Heat the mixture until the chips are hot.
4. Finally, drizzle sweet chilli sauce over the chips, gently mixing it in. Serve the dish sprinkled with fresh coriander/cilantro and spring onions.

SAVOURY - HULL PATTY

Ingredients:

- 4 large potatoes
- 1/2 tsp dried sage
- 1/4 tsp ground black pepper
- 120g/1 cup plain/all-purpose flour
- 2 eggs, beaten
- 200ml/ 3/4 cup cold water

Instructions:

1. Peel the potatoes and cut them into even chunks.
2. Boil the potatoes in lightly salted water until soft and fully cooked.
3. Drain the potatoes and allow them to cool slightly before mashing them in a large bowl.
4. Season the mashed potatoes with dried sage and pepper. Mix well.
5. Once the mixture has cooled enough to handle, shape it into palm-sized patties about 4 cm/ 1 1/2 inch thick.
6. Mix the flour with the beaten eggs and water in a separate bowl. Whisk until the batter is smooth. Season with a pinch of sea salt.
7. Use a deep-frying method of your choice. Heat the oil/fat to 180C/370F.
8. Coat them in the batter, and carefully lower them into the hot oil/fat.
9. Remove them once they turn golden brown.
10. Let them drain on a rack and serve while still warm.

S H A D   D A B

Ingredients:

- 4 scallops. Prepare the scallops. (potato scallop - dab) Recipe in this book)
- 4 burger buns (also known as baps, barmcakes, etc.).
- Mayonnaise, to taste.
- Enough iceberg lettuce to form a thick layer on each burger bun.
- Sufficient slices of cheese of your choice to add a layer to the burger buns.

Instructions:

1. Prepare and cook 4 large potato scallops according to the recipe in this book.
2. Slice open the buns and butter each side.
3. Add a thick layer of lettuce to the bottom half.
4. Add a layer of cheese of your choice.
5. Place a potato scallop on top.
6. Add mayonnaise to taste.
7. Season with salt to taste.
8. Top with the other half of the bun.

SMACK BARM

Ingredients:

- Create 1 large battered potato scallop to the potato scallop (dab) recipe in this book
- Provide 1 barmcake (bap, burger bun, etc) for each of the potato scallops
- Purchase enough mushy peas for 2 tbsp for each potato scallop to be served, or use the mushy peas recipe in this book. Keep any pea liquid
- Butter

Instructions:

1. Other than the bread, each item should be cooked and hot at this stage.
2. Halve the barmcakes and butter each side. Place a potato scallop on each barmcake.
3. Add 2 tablespoons of mushy peas to each potato scallop.
4. If available, spoon some pea juice (also known as pea wet) over the potato scallops topped with mushy peas.
5. Cover with the other half of the barmcake and serve.

TWICE FRIED CHIPPY CHIPS

Ingredients:

- 900g/2lb Maris Piper or King Edwards or similar

Instructions:

STAGE ONE

1. Peel and cut the potatoes into finger-sized pieces. Use the offcuts, reshape them as necessary, and remove as much surface moisture as possible.
2. Choose your preferred method of deep frying.
3. Heat the oil/fat to 150C/300F. Test the oil/fat's readiness by dropping a chip into it; it is ready when it floats and bubbles appear around the edges.
4. Gently lower the chips into the oil/fat using a large metal sieve or basket.
5. Cook for about 10 minutes or until they are tender but not browned. This stage is for blanching rather than fully cooking the chips.
6. Transfer them to a tray or bowl to cool down to room temperature.

STAGE TWO

- Increase the oil/fat temperature to 180C/370F and test it again by frying a single room-temperature blanched chip.
- Once it floats to the surface, begin cooking the rest in servings, but avoid overcrowding as this can cause the oil/fat temperature to drop too quickly.
- Fry until they reach a golden colour and test a chip to ensure it is crispy on the outside and soft and fluffy on the inside.
- Transfer them to kitchen paper/towel to remove excess oil/fat.

BEER BATTER

1. Choose one of the batters created for the fish, and choose a light batter, like soda/sparkling water, vinegar, or tempura
2. Prepare the batter while the chips are cooling to room temperature after being cooked at 140C/300F.
3. Turn up the oil/fat to 180C/370F.
4. Coat the chips lightly in the batter and lower them gently into the oil/fat.
5. They are cooked when they float and are golden and crispy and soft inside.

BANANA - BATTERED

Ingredients:

- Choose one of the batters created for the fish, and choose a light batter, like soda/sparkling water, vinegar, or tempura
- 8 bananas, halved lengthways
- 60g/ 1/2 cup plain/all-purpose flour for dredging
- 1 tbsp sugar of choice

Instructions:

1. Create the batter.
2. Use a deep frying method of choice. Heat the oil/fat to 180C/370F.
3. Dredge the sliced bananas in the flour before coating them in the batter.
4. Carefully lower them into the hot oil/fat. Remove them once they turn a light golden, which could be as soon as a minute or two, as the banana takes little time to cook. After frying, sprinkle lightly with sugar on the top surfaces, and let them drain on a rack and serve while still warm.

M A R S   B A R S   -   B A T T E R

Ingredients:

- Choose one of the batters created for the fish, and choose a heavy batter, like beer, but not soda/sparkling water, vinegar, or tempura. Also, you might need to half the quantity of the batter ingredients

- 4 to 6 Mars Bars, or 10 to 14 half-sized bars

Instructions:

1. Create the batter.
2. Arrange the fish on a baking tray lined with kitchen paper and dab thoroughly to remove excess moisture.
3. Use a deep frying method of choice. Heat the oil/fat to 180C/370F. Dip each Mars Bar into the batter, gently lower them into the oil/fat, and fry until they turn golden.
4. It is only about cooking the batter. The Mars Bar will melt in the hot batter a little in the oil/fat and more when removed from the fryer, so remove them as soon as the batter is cooked. Let them drain on a rack and serve while still warm.

PINEAPPLE FRITTER

Ingredients:

- Choose one of the batters created for the fish, and choose a light batter, like soda/sparkling water, vinegar, or tempura
- 1 fresh pineapple, peeled, cored and sliced into rings
- 1 tbsp granulated sugar for dusting
- 60g/ 1/2 cup plain/all-purpose flour for dredging

Instructions:

1. Create the batter.
2. Use a deep frying method of choice. Heat the oil/fat to 180C/370F.
3. Thoroughly dry the pineapple rings with kitchen roll/towel.
4. Dredge the pineapple rings in the flour, patting the flower on in a thin layer, then coat them in the batter.
5. Carefully lower them into the hot oil/fat. Remove them once they turn golden brown.
6. Let them drain on a rack and serve while still warm.
7. Dust the fritters lightly with the sugar.

B B Q   S A U C E

Ingredients:

- 220g/1 cup brown sugar
- 15ml/1 tbsp Worcestershire sauce
- 60ml/ 1/4 cup apple cider vinegar
- 1/2 tsp sea salt
- 1/2 tsp ground black pepper
- 1 tsp onion powder
- 250ml/1 cup tomato ketchup
- 1/2 tsp paprika

Instructions:

1. In a small saucepan, mix all the ingredients and place it over medium heat.
2. Once it reaches a boil, lower the heat to a simmer.
3. Continue to cook for 15 minutes, stirring from time to time.

BEEF GRAVY

Ingredients:

- 50ml/2 cups beef broth or stock
- 1 beef stock cube or 5 ml/1 tsp liquid bouillon
- 60g/2 oz butter
- Sea salt and black pepper to taste
- 1/2 tsp garlic powder
- 1/2 tsp onion powder
- 60g/ 1/2 cup plain/all-purpose flour

Instructions:

1. Combine the butter and flour in a saucepan over medium heat, stirring consistently to create a roux (thickener).
2. Gradually introduce half of the beef broth or stock, whisking briskly to ensure a smooth, lump-free mixture.
3. Then, add the remaining beef broth with onion powder, garlic powder, and beef stock cube or bouillon.
4. Allow the gravy to boil until it achieves a thick and smooth consistency.
5. Finally, adjust the seasoning with salt and pepper to taste.

CHEESE SAUCE

Ingredients:

- 120g/4 oz mature cheddar, grated/shredded
- 60g/2 oz unsalted butter
- 30g/ 1/4 cup plain/all-purpose flour
- 400ml/ 1 1/2 cups whole/full-fat milk

Instructions:

1. Combine the milk, flour, and butter in a saucepan. Place the saucepan over medium heat and whisk vigorously.
2. Continue whisking as the butter melts, the flour dissolves, and the mixture as it comes to a boil. Once at a boil, keep whisking for a couple of minutes.
3. Finally, incorporate the grated/shredded mature cheddar cheese until it melts into the mixture. If the sauce is too thick for your liking, add a little more milk. If it is too thin, add more flour or cheese and mix well.

CHIPPY CURRY SAUCE

Ingredients:

- 2 tbsp cornflour/cornstarch
- 30ml/2 tbsp malt vinegar
- 1 tsp turmeric
- 2 garlic cloves, chopped
- 1 large onion, peeled, chopped
- 2 tbsp currants or raisins
- 2 tbsp mild curry powder
- 1 tbsp fresh ginger, peeled, chopped
- 500ml/2 cups chicken or vegetable stock or broth

Instructions:

1. Melt the butter in a large saucepan over medium-low heat.
2. Add onions, garlic, and ginger, and fry them for 10 minutes or until soft but not brown.
3. Mix in the curry powder, turmeric, currants/raisins, and vinegar, and cook for another minute.
4. Pour in the stock and bring to a boil, then reduce to a simmer for 30 minutes, stirring to prevent it from sticking.
5. Dissolve the cornflour/cornstarch into a little water and stir it into the sauce.
6. Remove the mixture from the saucepan and blend it in a food processor or blender before returning it to the pan.
7. Simmer, constantly stirring, until the sauce has thickened and is silky.

For a fruity curry, instead of blending the raisins/sultanas and ginger, finely chop the raisins/sultanas and coarsely grate/shred to the ginger, and add 2 tbsp of apple sauce at step 2.

HOLLANDAISE SAUCE

Ingredients:

- 1/4 tsp cayenne pepper
- 1/4 tsp sea salt
- 3 egg yolks
- 1 tsp freshly squeezed lemon juice
- 30ml/2 tbsp water, room temperature
- 1/2 tsp Dijon mustard
- 120g/4 oz butter

Instructions:

1. Separate the yolks from the whites of the eggs, reserving the whites in a sealed container in the refrigerator for use in another dish within a couple of days.
2. Combine the egg yolks in a small saucepan with the water, lemon juice, and Dijon mustard, whisking them together.
3. Cut the butter into small chunks and stir them into the yolk mixture. Heat the saucepan over a medium-low setting, continuously whisking.
4. As the butter begins to melt, the mixture may foam slightly. Keep whisking for approximately 3 minutes or until the sauce thickens, then promptly remove from the heat. It should have a consistency that can coat the back of a spoon.
5. Season with salt and cayenne pepper to your liking. The sauce can be served immediately or covered to retain warmth. Whisk in a teaspoon of warm water to thin it if it becomes overly thick.

HORSERADISH CREAM

Ingredients:

- Prepared horseradish sauce
- Soured/sour cream
- Apple cider vinegar
- Mayonnaise
- Pinch of sea salt and black pepper
- Chives, finely chopped

Instructions:

1. Mix all the ingredients in a small bowl. You may serve it immediately or store it in a covered container in the fridge for up to one week.

IRISH CURRY SAUCE

Ingredients:

- 1 unrefrigerated tomato
- 2 tsp curry powder
- 1 onion, peeled
- 250ml/1 cup vegetable stock or broth
- 1 small green apple, peeled
- 1 tbsp onion chutney
- 2 tbsp plain/all-purpose flour
- 30g/1 oz butter

Instructions:

1. Blend the tomato, onion, apple and chutney.
2. Heat the butter over medium heat and fry the tomato, onion, apple, and chutney mixture in a pan until it turns brown, but do not allow it to burn.
3. Reduce the mixture to a simmer and blend in the flour and curry powder.
4. Slowly add the stock or broth, whisking continuously.
5. Bring the mixture to a boil, removing any foam on the surface.
6. Once at a boil, cover the pan and let it simmer for about 30 minutes, ensuring it doesn't burn or stick to the pan.
7. Season the sauce with salt to taste.

MUSHROOM GRAVY

Ingredients:

- 500ml/2 cups vegetable broth or stock
- 1 onion, peeled, finely chopped
- 450g/1 lb Cremini or white mushrooms, sliced
- 10ml/2 tsp Tamari sauce
- 1 garlic clove, grated/shredded
- 30g/ 1/4 cup plain/all-purpose flour
- 1 tbsp fresh parsley, finely chopped
- Sea salt and ground pepper to taste
- 30ml/2 tbsp olive oil

Instructions:

1. Warm the olive oil over medium heat in a large frying pan/skillet. Saute the onion until tender.
2. Add the mushrooms and continue cooking until they soften.
3. Add tamari, garlic, and parsley to the mixture, followed by sprinkling over the flour. Stir consistently for about a minute.
4. Pour in the broth and allow the mixture to simmer until it thickens, whisking frequently. This could take some time.
5. Finalise by seasoning with salt and pepper to taste.

ONION GRAVY

Ingredients:

- Sea salt and black pepper to taste
- 30ml/2 tbsp Worcestershire sauce
- 15ml/1 tbsp olive oil
- 2 onions, peeled, sliced
- 1/2 tsp dried thyme
- 1 tsp Dijon mustard
- 400ml/ 1 1/2 cups beef broth or stock
- 1 tbsp plain/all-purpose flour
- 1 tbsp fresh parsley, finely chopped

Instructions:

1. Warm the oil over low heat in a saucepan and saute the onions until they soften.
2. Increase the heat to medium, add a little broth or stock, and stir in the flour.
3. Gradually introduce the beef broth or stock while continually stirring.
4. Incorporate mustard, thyme, Worcestershire sauce, and season with salt and pepper.
5. Allow the mixture to simmer until it reaches your desired consistency.
6. Garnish with parsley.

SEAFOOD SAUCE

Ingredients:

- 1/2 tsp hot sauce of choice
- 15ml/1 tbsp freshly squeezed lemon juice
- 15ml/1 tbsp tomato ketchup
- 1/2 tsp paprika
- 125ml/ 1/2 cup mayonnaise
- 1/4 tsp garlic powder
- 1 tsp Worcestershire sauce

Instructions:

1. Mix all the ingredients in a small bowl. You may serve it immediately or store it in a covered container in the fridge for up to one week.

TARTAR SAUCE

Ingredients:

- 250ml/1 cup mayonnaise
- 1 tsp freshly squeezed lemon juice
- 1/2 tsp Dijon mustard
- 1 tbsp sweet green relish or sweet pickle relish

Instructions:

1. Finely chop the relish and combine it with the other ingredients in a bowl.
2. Stir thoroughly and serve.

VEGAN AND GLUTEN FREE GRAVY

Ingredients:

- 1 tsp Dijon mustard
- 1 small onion, grated/shredded
- 15ml/1 tbsp Tamari sauce
- 30g/ 1/4 cup rice flour
- 30g/ 3 tbsp nutritional yeast
- 500ml/2 cups vegetable broth or stock

Instructions:

1. Combine all the ingredients in a medium-sized saucepan and bring the mixture to a boil.
2. Once brought to a boil, reduce the heat to medium and whisk for a few minutes until the gravy reaches your desired thickness.
3. It can be stored in a sealed container in the fridge for up to a week.

Notes & Recipes

Notes & Recipes

Printed in Dunstable, United Kingdom

71011820R00057